Father-Words
for You, too

Father-Words
for You, too

THE WORD
The Universal Spirit

Second Edition, 2000

Gabriele Publishing House
P.O. Box 2221, Deering, NH 03244
(844) 576-0937
WhatsApp/Messenger: +49 151 1883 8742
www.Gabriele-Publishing-House.com

Licensed edition
translated from the original German title:
"Vaterworte auch an Dich"
Order No. S 108en

From the Universal Life Series
with the consent of
© Verlag DAS WORT GmbH
im Universellen Leben
Max-Braun-Str. 2
97828 Marktheidenfeld/Altfeld
Germany

ISBN 1-890841-16-1

Preface

Words of guidance.

Words from the eternal universal life, from the source of truth, the fullness of the all-power, from the highest consciousness of the universe.

With this book we are privileged to share in the personal words of the Father for His child. These words are also directed to us, to accept and receive in us.

God, the universal spirit, the Father of us all, from whom we have removed ourselves in self-will, who loves us unchangeably and who longs for each one of us, speaks to us unceasingly, in the depth of our infinitely eternal being. When we have set out on the inner mystical path and have climbed some steps of evolution to higher spirituality, then we, too, shall hear the word of the Spirit in our own inner being.

The stream of the divine will then flow into our brain cells by way of the core of being of our soul and through the largely purified areas of our soul. Having been cleansed of human ideas and opinions, the brain cells serve Him as an instrument.

The spirit of God, the divine consciousness, then communicates purely and clearly with us in the "I Am." These revelations of the spirit of God via the inner word are meant only for the child; they are not the prophetic word.

When God speaks through a prophet, the word is more than the inner word of the individual on the last steps of his path to God. The prophetic word means that the spirit of God speaks through soul and person. This word from the Father, which streams purely through soul and body, is not meant only for the prophet, but for all people who are open for it.

According to the will of the Lord, His prophetess who is our sister Gabriele, lets us share in the gifts coming from the spirit of God, which she was privileged to receive as His child. Let us accept thankfully what the Almighty wants to say to us, too.

The Original Christians
in Universal Life

I Am with you

Come to Me at every moment.

Talk everything over with your Father whose spirit dwells in you. I, the life, want to lead and guide you.

For wherever you are, there Am I, for I dwell in you and in all Being.

Let your heart continuously radiate love, then you are linked with Me, with the One who I Am in all forms of life, the spirit of your Father.

Do not fear

I, your Father, Am the love. You came forth out of My eternal consciousness. The consciousness of eternal life is also your life.

See, you do not die. What should die is your human ego, your passions and base tendencies. The more they die, the more I will resurrect in you.

If I Am consciously resurrected in you and you become aware of Me, then you truly live. I will resurrect in the one who resurrects in Me and he will be with Me consciously, and I with him.

This, My child, is the true life, far from oppressing fear, from sin and death.

Do not sin

My child, sin is against your heavenly Father.

Everything that does not correspond to My holy law is sinful.

The one who loves Me keeps My commandments; he fulfills the law of life.

When you truly love Me, you will see to it that your feelings, thoughts and words are pure, that your actions are good and your life selfless.

Then your being will be filled with light. The beauty of your inner being will then find expression externally.

You will gain in charm and spirituality.

Then you will become a being who is imbued with My sublime and noble light, with a light-force which irradiates, radiating through you and shedding its radiance on your neighbor.

This is the pure love, My child, which sets you free. Sin binds the soul and keeps it in the imprisonment of human thinking and wanting.

Divine love makes you free and beautiful.

It marks the person through the nobility of a pure soul.

*Become pure
and you will be free*

My child, the purity of the soul makes the person virtuous and good.

The one who loves, gives and the one who gives, becomes free. See, the giver is truly free from everything that is dear and precious to the taker. The giver has only to look into the countenance of the taker to understand what the latter needs. And so, give to the one who is in need and at the same time you are giving yourself to Me, the eternal Giver.

The Giver is very near to the one who gives; it is the love, which frees the soul from the ties of greed, envy and egoism.

My child, only the giving one has true freedom. Give and you will receive love and freedom from Me. In selfless giving, the selfless seeker finds the justice of the Father who knows how to protect and sustain His child.

Look at the sparrows; they do not gather and reap; they do not hoard in barns, yet they are maintained and are free through the giving, all-just Spirit.

Look at the lilies in the fields, they flourish without asking why it rains and whence the waters flow which give them to drink.

See, they sense the all-justice, the giving life, the I Am in all Being.

Be just in yourself

I Am the love, the all-just Spirit. Become just in yourself and you will find your way to Me, the love.

See, I lead you by way of your base feelings and thoughts, by way of your words that often do not correspond to your feelings and thoughts. How often does a person speak other than he thinks. This is hypocrisy and not honest. See, My child, in this lies the conflict which does not let the person become free and loving. The hypocrite is not clever; he wants to cover up that which is nevertheless evident to Me before My eyes. Although he has put himself in the best light before his neighbor for the moment, the One who knows all things will let all things become evident according to the law of sowing and reaping.

Be just in yourself. Speak only what you feel and think. If you have made this a part of you, then, My child, you will observe yourself more and more each day and you will surrender everything that is impure to the eradicating light of your Father, so that your inner attitude may become noble and your feelings and thoughts good.

If your inner attitude is noble, you will speak only what is noble and good. Because when your attitude shapes your feelings and thoughts, then your feelings and thoughts are the same as your words.

See, this is being just in yourself.

A good attitude leads to a good social and commercial life

The person who thinks only good and noble things will also engage in fair trade. See, My child, in the temporal there are business transactions, but not in the eternal life.

A person needs many a thing which the soul has already long since possessed as a gift from the Giver of eternal life.

A person needs food and clothing, shelter and many other things. The soul which possesses the wealth of the heavens in itself must often patiently endure what the shell, the person, needs, what he strives for and aspires to.

Selfless business transactions contain at the same time a positive way of life. The one who carries out trade in the spirit of selfless love will also walk in Me, the all-justice.

See, only a person who is noble and pure and is like Me, the Eternal, has a clear conscience. A good attitude during his sojourn in time sets person and soul free.

Freedom

My child, to be free means to be free from oneself.

What does being free mean? When a person's striving and aspiration is to please only God, he will not make the opinion of his neighbor his own. He will not make the longings and desires of his neighbor his own. His longing consists in pleasing God, so that he will grow ever closer to Me, the Eternal.

See, in self-complacency lies overestimation, overvaluation of one's own person. This results in a human kind of contentment. But this self-satisfaction brings the spiritual life to a standstill, thus producing confinement and lack of freedom.

May the one who wants to be free look only to Me and and be single-minded in the spirit. May he not be lukewarm. To be lukewarm is to fall away from Me and opens the door for personal-istic thinking.

To be free means to be one with Me in word and in deed. This is truly the seed that brings a good harvest both for the God-man and for his neighbor, My child.

A SIMPLE WAY TO PRAY

A SIMPLE WAY TO PRAY

Martin Luther

Foreword by Marjorie J. Thompson

WESTMINSTER JOHN KNOX PRESS
LOUISVILLE, KENTUCKY

Excerpt from Martin Luther, "A Simple Way to Pray," *Luther's Works*, Vol. 43: *Devotional Writings* II (Philadelphia: Fortress Press, 1968), 193–211. Used by permission of Augsburg Fortress Publishers.

Book design by Sharon Adams
Cover design by Pam Poll
Cover illustration by Antonio Rosario, The Image Bank

Published by Westminster John Knox Press
Louisville, Kentucky

This book is printed on acid-free paper that meets the American National Standards Institute Z39.48 standard. ♾

PRINTED IN THE UNITED STATES OF AMERICA

00 01 02 03 04 05 06 07 08 09 – 10 9 8 7 6 5 4 3 2 1

Library of Congress Cataloging-in-Publication Data

Luther, Martin, 1483–1546.
  [Einfältige Weise zu beten für einen guten Freund. English]
  A simple way to pray / Martin Luther.—1st ed.
    p. cm.
  Includes bibliographical references.
  ISBN 0-664-22273-0 (alk. paper)
  1. Prayer—Christianity—Early works to 1800. I. Title.

BV215.L8813 2000
248.3'2—dc21   00-029015

The good seed

My child, the true life is giving.

Therefore, to give is better than to take.
To give sets soul and person free.

In giving is relinquishment, self-sacri-
fice, the sacrifice of all that is dear and
precious to the person.

See, the selfless gift in word and deed
is the good seed that will bear fruit.
The fruit will not be given back to the
earth, for a ripe fruit always finds its
taker. It is the spirit of life, which har-
vests the ripe fruit and brings it into the
land of maturity, the land of eternity,
where only fully matured life has a
place.

Become ripened fruit

The one who wants to mature on the tree of recognition must make sacrifices, not only for his own sake, but for the common good. For each bears the burden of the other.

The soul matures in self-recognition, My child.

Self-recognition and the sacrifice of your self are not sufficient to enable you to enter the Father-house.

Only the voluntary sacrifice of love for one's neighbor, the voluntary, selfless deed of love, in service, opens for the soul the door to eternal consciousness, to Me, to the One, who I Am, the life.

Contents

The sacrifice of love for one's neighbor

The sacrifice of love done in the right deed is true life. It frees the soul from the shackles of its ego. Through this, person and soul find access to all those hearts which truly seek Me.

A sacrifice of love means to give your self up, to think no more of yourself, to no longer demand or crave, to give your-self only to God and to your neighbor. This is true sacrifice; this is the great-ness of consciousness.

The one who surrenders himself self-lessly gains more than he can ever imagine. I will be with him and give him what he needs and what is neces-sary for the redemption of his soul.

True greatness

My child, greatness is shown only by the one who forgets himself. And the one who has forgotten his self is great.

How small and lowly is the human ego, the person, whose thinking and acting revolve only around his own concerns, who is worried solely about his own welfare.

See, whatever you think and do today are the seeds for tomorrow.

Therefore, the rich person who strives only for his welfare and his possessions will, depending on his way of life, gradually lose everything until he has become so poor in body and soul that

Foreword

We know that when children ask us how to pray, it is rarely an abstract question. They want to know how we ourselves pray. The same was surely true for those first disciples who longed to understand Jesus' prayer life, the power of which was so evident to them. It was in this manner that Martin Luther interpreted the request of his friend and barber, Peter, when he undertook to explain his personal prayer practice in these pages.

Luther includes a few general instructions similar to those of other spiritual writers: the best times of day for prayer, postures and gestures conducive to prayer, aiming for depth and sincerity rather than burdening oneself with length. But this is emphatically not a treatise *about* prayer. It is an illustrated guide whose illustrations are composed of actual prayers.

There is a disarmingly childlike quality to this treatise. As if taking a little one's hand to guide the pencil in writing, Luther assumes no particular background or experience and records with great specificity sample prayers in his own style. He makes it clear that his actual words are not to be followed by rote. Indeed, such "parroting" of written prayers was one of his deeply held grievances against the Roman Church. Luther is simply illustrating by example how one might pray in a way that is consistent with Reformation teachings.

Yet Luther's habitual form of prayer is deeply rooted in historic Catholic practices that were no doubt as familiar as the air he breathed. Turning to scripture (particularly the Psalms and the Gospels) as a way to "warm the heart" in preparation for prayer expresses a very ancient wisdom in the church. Moreover, Luther's basic pattern of meditating on each phrase of the Lord's Prayer has rich affinities with the Benedictine tradition of *lectio divina*. The pattern is essentially one of drawing out the meaning of a he must beg for his daily bread, or work very hard for it.

Each one receives, My child, according to the way he thinks and behaves.

Receive the highest

The one who wants to receive the highest, Me, the all-power and the fullness, must lose himself, must give himself.

See, rich is only the one who sacrifices his personal ego for the good of mankind. My child, he will not live in the gutter nor must he live there, because he receives from My fullness and attains what is due to him as the child of his Father.

He will receive everything he needs and more, in accordance with the natural laws of this earth.

True wealth

True wealth is the radiance of your soul which perceives in itself the holy eternal Spirit, which is one with Me, the great primordial Spirit. This child will not live in need; it will receive from My hands and partake of the great feast of life—not only in heaven, but already on earth.

What do you lack, My child? You are not rich externally—as the rich of this world; you possess inner wealth. Whatever you need in your outer life, I have given to you, and more.

See, the children of the kingdom of spiritual life live in the fullness. People receive what they need and more, depending on the inner radiance of their soul. A human being cannot be given the complete fullness of the eternal homeland, because the earth is dense and thus constricted by time and space. Many people live in this space and in time, and thus the planet earth is over-populated. However, the one who awakens the inner radiance through a life in Me will also have enough on earth and will not want for anything.

given phrase in our own understanding and experience, paraphrasing, interpreting, and expanding upon it so as to make the prayer our own by affirmation and assent. We meditate in this fashion until the Holy Spirit comes and leads us into mysteries of faith we could neither imagine nor devise. This is fundamentally the movement from active to passive meditation (sometimes called contemplation) in the classic spiritual tradition of the church.

The path of Luther's prayer is instructive. He begins with the Lord's Prayer, and continues (if time and inclination allow) with the Ten Commandments and the Apostles' Creed, devising a "fourfold garland" of meditation and prayer for the latter two. In the early church, candidates for baptism received instruction based on the creed they would confess, the Ten Commandments, and other sources of guidance. This practice was lost during the Middle Ages, but revived in the

Reformation era through distinctive forms of catechetical instruction. The structure of Creed, Commandments, and Lord's Prayer governs most of these, including the new Study Catechism approved for use in 1998 by the 210th General Assembly of the Presbyterian Church (U.S.A.).

Since meditation on any passage of scripture or creed involves associations relevant to personal and historical context, we see many elements of Luther's doctrine and teaching embedded in this text. Reformation "bones of contention" poke right through the skin of these prayers! The treatise was written well after Luther had formulated a series of sermons on which instruction for his Larger and Smaller Catechisms was based. Many of the same thoughts are presented here. The fusion of theology and prayer is especially evident in his treatment of the Apostles' Creed. This is as it should be. Not only is the Creed a distillation of essential church doctrine, but Martin Luther was an embodiment of the wisdom expressed by Evagrius Ponticus in the fourth century: "A theologian is one whose prayer is true."

We will naturally find aspects of Luther's controversy with Rome outdated, yet the essence of his teaching on prayer remains timeless. He reveals how prayer takes us beyond the literal sense of a passage to its deeper meanings and broader applications. He comprehends with acuity how inattention in prayer dishonors God's gracious presence, making as strong a case for mental alertness as any modern proponent of "awareness" in meditation. He commends the practice of emphasizing a single word while meditating on the essentials of our faith, in order to heighten varied accents of meaning. And he understands the certainty of faith expressed in that simple closing word of prayer, "Amen."

Luther once acknowledged that he "could not get on" without three or four hours of prayer daily. Few of us are possessed of his prodigious energy and commitment, but the authenticity of his prayer life should encourage us to attend to what we may learn from his knowledge and experience in faith. He himself once wrote, "None can believe how powerful prayer is, and what it is able to effect, but those who have learned it by experience." May we find grace in discovering and deepening this truth.

MARJORIE J. THOMPSON

Epiphany, 2000

I, the Giver

My child, become My conscious image!

See, My love streams eternally! I give the forces of love untiringly to the great totality. All entities receive My power according to their consciousness. Each one may take from the stream of love, but each can take only as much as corresponds to its consciousness.

The consciousness of all entities can be compared to a flower calyx. The more the calyx opens and turns toward the sun, the more rays of the sun will enter into the calyx. See, My child, the more a person opens for My love, that is, the more selfless he becomes, the more forces he will receive from My salvation and My life-bringing power.

Love always gives equally. Love streams for all Being: for spirit beings, humans, souls, animals, plants and stones. All Being receives.

The more selfless and radiating your nature becomes, the more you can receive and give from My wellspring.

Experience, My child that to give is better than to take! The one who gives selflessly receives abundantly from the source of eternal love.

I Am the love

I Am the absolute love.

I see you solely as a perfect child of My love. The imperfections will lighten and dissolve through the power of the law of cause and effect, but not the absolute love.

My child, become My image! Look at your fellow man only from My consciousness of perfect love! See them as perfect beings! Do not look at their faults and shortcomings! Forgive!

Someone who beholds in everything only the perfect, the beautiful and the noble sees all of this with the eyes of love. And the one who views everything through My love will become truly noble and loving.

Kindness, friendliness and love draw into such a person. He is the one who could change the world for the better, insofar as the world would listen to him and would examine and follow up on his experiences.

Publisher's Note

Luther was asked by his barber, Peter Besk-endorf, for some practical guidance on how to compose oneself for prayer. Luther complied with this request by writing this brief treatise, which was published in the spring of 1535 under the title A *Simple Way to Pray, for a Good Friend*. It is counted a classic in the devotional literature of Protestantism.

It should be noted that Luther always begins with a passage from the Bible or the Creed. First, he carefully reflects upon the content of the passage and then meditates upon what the Holy Spirit is saying to him personally in and through the passage.

A Simple Way to Pray,
For a Good Friend,
Peter, the Master Barber

A Simple Way to Pray

Dear Master Peter: I will tell you as best I can what I do personally when I pray. May our dear Lord grant to you and to everybody to do it better than I! Amen.

First, when I feel that I have become cool and joyless in prayer because of other tasks or thoughts (for the flesh and the devil always impede and obstruct prayer), I take my little psalter, hurry to my room, or, if it be the day and hour for it, to the church where a congregation is assembled and, as time permits, I say quietly to myself and word-for-word the Ten Commandments, the Creed, and, if I have time, some words of Christ or of Paul, or some psalms, just as a child might do.

It is a good thing to let prayer be the first business of the morning and the last at night. Guard yourself carefully against those false, deluding ideas which tell you, "Wait a little while. I will pray in an hour; first I must attend to this or that." Such thoughts get you away from prayer into other affairs which so hold your attention and involve you that nothing comes of prayer for that day.

It may well be that you may have some tasks which are as good or better than prayer, especially in an emergency. There is a saying ascribed to <u>St. Jero</u>me that everything a believer does is prayer[1] and a proverb, "He <u>who works faithfully prays twice</u>." This can be said because a believer fears and honors God in his work and remembers the command- ment not to wrong anyone, or to try to steal, defraud, or cheat. Such thoughts and such faith undoubtedly transform his work into prayer and a sacrifice of praise.

On the other hand it is also true that the work of an unbeliever is outright cursing and so he who works faithlessly curses twice. While he does his work his thoughts are occupied with a neglect of God and violation of his law, how to take advantage of his neighbor, how to steal from him and defraud him. What else can such thoughts be but out and out curses against God and man, which makes one's work and effort a double curse by which a man curses himself. In the end they are beggars and bunglers. It is of such continual prayer that Christ says in Luke 11, "Pray without ceasing,"[2] because one must unceasingly guard against sin and wrong-doing, something one cannot do unless one fears God and keeps his commandment in mind, as Psalm 1 [1, 2] says, "Blessed is he who meditates upon his law day and night."

Yet we must be careful not to break the habit of true prayer and imagine other works to be necessary which, after all, are nothing of the kind. Thus at the end we become lax and lazy, cool and listless toward prayer. The devil who besets us is not lazy or careless, and our flesh is too ready and eager to sin and is disinclined to the spirit of prayer.

When your heart has been warmed by such recitation to yourself [of the Ten Commandments, the words of Christ, etc.] and is intent upon the matter, kneel or stand with your hands folded and your eyes toward heaven and speak or think as briefly as you can:

O Heavenly Father, dear God, I am a poor unworthy sinner. I do not deserve to raise my eyes or hands toward thee or to pray. But because thou hast commanded us all to pray and hast promised to hear us and through thy dear Son Jesus Christ hast taught us both how and what to pray, I come to thee in obedience to thy word, trusting in thy gracious promise. I pray in the name of my Lord Jesus Christ together with all thy saints and Christians on earth as he has taught us: Our Father who art, etc., through the whole prayer, word for word.

Then repeat one part or as much as you wish, perhaps the first petition: "Hallowed be thy name," and say: "Yes, Lord God, dear Father, hallowed be thy name, both in us and throughout the whole world. Destroy and root out the abominations, idolatry, and heresy of the Turk, the pope, and all false teachers and fanatics who wrongly use thy name and in scandalous ways take it in vain,[3] and horribly blaspheme it. They insistently boast that they teach thy word and the laws of the church, though they really use the devil's deceit and trickery in thy name to wretchedly seduce many poor souls throughout the world, even killing and shedding much innocent blood, and in such persecution they believe that they render thee a divine service.

Dear Lord God, convert and restrain [them]. Convert those who are still to be converted that they with us and we with them may hallow and praise thy name, both with true and pure doctrine and with a good and holy life. Restrain those who are unwilling to be converted so that they be forced to cease from misusing, defiling, and dishonoring thy holy name and from misleading the poor people. Amen."

The second petition: "Thy kingdom come." Say: "O dear Lord, God and Father, thou seest how worldly wisdom and reason not only profane thy name and ascribe the honor due to thee to lies and to the devil, but how they also take the power, might, wealth and glory which thou hast given them on earth for ruling the world and thus serving thee, and use it in their own ambition to oppose thy kingdom. They are many and mighty; they plague and hinder the tiny flock of thy kingdom who are weak, despised, and few. They will not tolerate thy flock on earth and think that by plaguing them they render a great and godly service to thee. Dear Lord, God and Father, convert them and defend us. Convert those who are still to become children and members of thy kingdom so that they with us and we with them may serve thee in thy kingdom in true faith and unfeigned love and that from thy kingdom which has begun, we may enter into thy eternal kingdom. Defend us against those who will not turn away their might and power from the destruction of thy kingdom so that when they are cast down from their thrones and humbled, they will have to cease from their efforts. Amen."

The third petition: "Thy will be done on earth as it is in heaven." Say: "O dear Lord, God and Father, thou knowest that the world, if it cannot destroy thy name or root out thy kingdom, is busy day and night with wicked tricks and schemes, strange conspiracies and intrigue, huddling together in secret counsel, giving mutual encouragement and support, raging and threatening and going about with every evil intention to destroy thy name, word, kingdom, and children. Therefore, dear Lord, God and Father, convert them and defend us. Convert those who have yet to acknowledge thy good will that they with us and we with them may obey thy will and for thy sake gladly, patiently, and joyously bear every evil, cross, and adversity, and thereby acknowledge, test, and experience thy benign, gracious, and perfect will. But defend us against those who in their rage, fury, hate, threats, and evil desires do not cease to do us harm. Make their wicked schemes, tricks, and devices to come to nothing so that these may be turned against them, as we sing in Psalm 7 [16]."[4]

The fourth petition: "Give us this day our daily bread." Say "Dear Lord, God and Father, grant us thy blessing also in this temporal and physical life. Graciously grant us blessed peace. Protect us against war and disorder. Grant to our dear emperor fortune and success against his enemies. Grant him wisdom and understanding to rule over his earthly kingdom in peace and prosperity. Grant to all kings, princes, and rulers good counsel and the will to preserve their domains and their subjects in tranquillity and justice. Especially aid and guide our dear prince N., under whose protection and shelter thou dost maintain us, so that he may be protected against all harm and reign blessedly, secure from evil tongues and disloyal people. Grant to all his subjects grace to serve him loyally and obediently. Grant to every estate—townsman or farmer—to be diligent and to display charity and loyalty toward each other. Give us favorable weather and good harvest. I commend to thee my house and property, wife and child. Grant that I may manage them well, supporting and educating them as a Christian should. Defend us against the Destroyer and all his wicked angels who would do us harm and mischief in this life. Amen."

The fifth petition: "Forgive us our trespasses as we forgive those who trespass against us." Say: "O dear Lord, God and Father, enter not into judgment against us because no man living is justified before thee. Do not count it against us as a sin that we are so unthankful for thine ineffable goodness, spiritual and physical, or that we stray into sin many times every day, more often than we can know or

recognize, Psalm 19 [12]. Do not look upon how good or how wicked we have been but only upon the infinite compassion which thou hast bestowed upon us in Christ, thy dear Son. Grant forgiveness also to those who have harmed or wronged us, as we forgive them from our hearts. They inflict the greatest injury upon themselves by arousing thy anger in their actions toward us. We are not helped by their ruin; we would much rather that they be saved with us. Amen." (Anyone who feels unable to forgive, let him ask for grace so that he can forgive; but that belongs in a sermon.)

The sixth petition: "And lead us not into temptation." Say: "O dear Lord, Father and God, keep us fit and alert, eager and diligent in thy word and service, so that we do not become complacent, lazy, and slothful as though we had already achieved everything. In that way the fearful devil cannot fall upon us, surprise us, and deprive us of thy precious word or stir up strife and factions among us and lead us into other sin and disgrace, both spiritually and physically. Rather grant us wisdom and strength through thy spirit that we may valiantly resist him and gain the victory. Amen."

The seventh petition: "But deliver us from evil." Say: "O dear Lord, God and Father, this wretched life is so full of misery and calamity, of danger and uncertainty, so full of malice and faithlessness (as St. Paul says, 'The days are evil' [Ephesians 5:16]) that we might rightfully grow weary of life and long for death. But thou, dear Father, knowest our frailty; therefore help us to pass in safety through so much wickedness and villainy; and, when our last hour comes, in thy mercy grant us a blessed departure from this vale of sorrows so that in the face of death we do not become fearful or despondent but in firm faith commit our souls into thy hands. Amen."

Finally, mark this, that you must always speak the Amen firmly. Never doubt that God in his mercy will surely hear you and say "yes" to your prayers. Never think that you are kneeling or standing alone, rather think that the whole of Christendom, all devout Christians, are standing there beside you and you are standing among them in a common, united petition which God cannot disdain. Do not leave your prayer without having said or thought, "Very well, God has heard my prayer; this I know as a certainty and a truth." That is what Amen means.

You should also know that I do not want you to recite all these words in your prayer. That would make it nothing but idle chatter and prattle, read word for word out of a book as were the rosaries by the laity and the prayers of the priests and monks. Rather do I want your heart to be stirred and guided concerning the thoughts which ought to be comprehended in the Lord's Prayer. These thoughts may be expressed, if your heart is rightly warmed and inclined toward prayer, in many different ways and with more words or fewer. I do not bind myself to such words or syllables, but say my prayers in one fashion today, in another tomorrow, depending upon my mood and feeling. I stay however, as nearly as I can, with the same general thoughts and ideas. It may happen occasionally that I may get lost among so many ideas in one petition that I forego the other six. If such an abundance of good thoughts comes to us we ought to disregard the other petitions, make room for such thoughts, listen in silence, and under no circumstances obstruct them. The Holy Spirit himself preaches here, and one word of his sermon is far better than a thousand of our prayers. Many times I have learned more from one prayer than I might have learned from much reading and speculation.

It is of great importance that the heart be made ready and eager for prayer. As the

Preacher says, "Prepare your heart for prayer, and do not tempt God" [Ecclesiasticus 18:23]. What else is it but tempting God when your mouth babbles and the mind wanders to other thoughts? Like the priest who prayed, "*Deus in adjutorium meum intende*.[5] Farmhand, did you unhitch the horses? *Domine ad adjuvandum me festina*.[6] Maid, go out and milk the cow. *Gloria patri et filio et spiritui sancto*.[7] Hurry up, boy, I wish the ague would take you!" I have heard many such prayers in my experience under the papacy; most of their prayers are of this sort. This is blasphemy and it would be better if they played at it if they cannot or do not care to do better. In my day I have prayed many such canonical hours myself, regrettably, and in such a manner that the psalm or the allotted time came to an end before I even realized whether I was at the beginning or in the middle.

Though not all of them blurt out the words as did the above mentioned cleric and mix business and prayer, they do it by the thoughts in their hearts. They jump from one thing to another in their thoughts and when it is all over they do not know what they have done or what they talked about. They start with *Laudate*[8] and right away they are in a fool's paradise. It seems to me that if someone could see what arises as prayer from a cold and unattentive heart he would conclude that he had never seen a more ridiculous kind of buffoonery. But, praise God, it is now clear to me that a person who forgets what he has said has not prayed well. In a good prayer one fully remembers every word and thought from the beginning to the end of the prayer.

So, a good and attentive barber keeps his thoughts, attention, and eyes on the razor and hair and does not forget how far he has gotten with his shaving or cutting. If he wants to engage in too much conversation or let his mind wander or look somewhere else he is likely to cut his customer's mouth, nose, or

Become My image

My child, beautiful is the life in Me and with Me!

Be of good cheer: hope, love and endure! See, the angels of the heavens are with you and with all My children who lift their hearts to Me and who daily cleanse their souls more and more of all the rubbish, of the trumpery of this world.

The one who strives toward the Highest will also receives from the Highest.

My child, be noble and good! Look steadfastly within and ask Me, your Lord and God, in all things. See, I will answer you according to your consciousness, for I Am everything in all things. Recognize this!

My child, follow My instructions, then you will grow and flourish daily ever more!

See, My love and My grace never forsake you. I, your Lord, lead you to the pinnacle of peace, where the eternal sun gives you only salvation and love.

Each soul particle needs My perfect light. If the many particles of the soul and the cells of your body are filled with light, then everything in you has been accomplished.

And so, you, too, are a cell of My body. See, it is luminous and bright; your being blossoms like the sunrise on the horizon of My life. Your senses live in Me, and I work through them; thus I Am in you consciously, everything in all things. See, may this knowledge give you strength and consolation during days full of work as well as during days full of deprivation.

The sun of righteousness is the delight of your soul. Thus, you may join in the song of praise of your soul, namely: I am in God, my Father, and my Father is consciously in me. I have found and feel the perfection of my soul, the spirit body, which has again become the image of my Father. Thanks be to You, O Lord, and to Your Son.

Give thanks in joy
and in sorrow

My child, learn to give the right thanks!

See, in true thankfulness lies infinite joy and selflessness. In true thankfulness, which rises from the depth of your soul to Me, the Eternal, lies true heroism. The one who gives thanks for everything, even in illness and in need, awakens in Me, the spirit of life.

Deep-felt thanks gives refreshment to soul and body. The person who gives thanks forgets himself. In truly forgetting yourself, My child, My strength awakens in you, which puts everything

in order and clears it up, which dissolves and wipes out much.

See, I am also mercy. Become merciful, and you will become a true servant of humanity.

True service

In forgetting oneself lies true heroism, true service.

The one who is a true servant of humanity does not think about money and goods. He sacrifices himself for his neighbor.

See, this is also true heroism; this is true greatness.

True heroism

A true hero is the one who gives everything, even his life, for his sheep. And so, My child, I have lived, loved and given, I, your Lord and Redeemer.

Now be brave and follow Me! Bear your cross courageously and know that I will carry your burden with you, if you entrust yourself to Me and if you surrender to Me all your faults and weaknesses and leave them in Me, the Christ-Spirit. Come, follow Me!

Follow Me

The one who follows Me can endure much, even the accusations and insults of his fellow man. The one who consciously enters into My following will not talk about the weaknesses and faults of his fellow man. Nor will he hold on to his still existing base characteristics and inclinations by brooding over them and being apprehensive.

The one who is in My following will always give, always give. He is the light in Me and I shine through him. In this way, he becomes capable of bearing much, and for many.

I Am the Good Shepherd. Be My sheep and become the lamb!

Become enduring

The suffering which you have to bear
at the moment are your own faults
which you have imposed upon your
soul during this or a former lifetime.
Now you may suffer through them.

Accept them and give thanks; for by
accepting and thanking you receive the
strength to endure what I cannot take
from you, since it is for the salvation
of your soul. My child, what remains
for you to endure gives you new rec-
ognitions on your path.

Endure, understand and mature; this
way you will mature toward Me and
you will blossom and reach full ripe-
ness. See, I pluck only fully ripened

fruit and carry it back into the glory, into the peace which the world does not know.

even his throat. Thus if anything is to be done well, it requires the full attention of all one's senses and members, as the proverb says, *"Pluribus intentus, minor est ad singula sensus"*— "He who thinks of many things, thinks of nothing and does nothing right." How much more does prayer call for concentration and singleness of heart if it is to be a good prayer!

This in short is the way I use the Lord's Prayer when I pray it. To this day I suckle at the Lord's Prayer like a child, and as an old man eat and drink from it and never get my fill. It is the very best prayer, even better than the psalter, which is so very dear to me. It is surely evident that a real master composed and taught it. What a great pity that the prayer of such a master is prattled and chattered so irreverently all over the world! How many pray the Lord's Prayer several thousand times in the course of a year, and if they were to keep on doing so for a thousand years they would not have tasted nor prayed one iota, one jot,[9] of it! In a word, the Lord's Prayer is the greatest martyr on earth (as are the name and word of God). Everybody tortures and abuses it; few take comfort and joy in its proper use.

If I have had time and opportunity to go through the Lord's Prayer, I do the same with the Ten Commandments. I take one part after another and free myself as much as possible from distractions in order to pray. I divide each commandment into four parts, thereby fashioning a garland of four strands. That is, I think of each commandment as, first, instruction, which is really what it is intended to be, and consider what the Lord God demands of me so earnestly. Second, I turn it into a thanksgiving; third, a confession; and fourth, a prayer. I do so in thoughts or words such as these:

"I am the Lord your God, etc. You shall have no other gods before me," etc. Here I earnestly consider that God expects and teaches me to trust him sincerely in all things and that it is his most earnest purpose to be my God. I must think of him in this way at the risk of losing eternal salvation. My heart must not build upon anything else or trust in any other thing, be it wealth, prestige, wisdom, might, piety, or anything else. Second, I give thanks for his infinite compassion by which he has come to me in such a fatherly way and, unasked, unbidden, and unmerited, has offered to be my God, to care for me, and to be my comfort, guardian, help, and strength in every time of need. We poor mortals have sought so many gods and would have to seek them still if he did not enable us to hear him openly tell us in our own language that he intends to be our God. How could we ever—in all eternity—thank him enough! Third, I confess and acknowledge my great sin and ingratitude for having so shamefully despised such sublime teachings and such a precious gift throughout my whole life, and for having fearfully provoked his wrath by countless acts of idolatry. I repent of these and ask for his grace. Fourth, I pray and say: "O my God and Lord, help me by thy grace to learn and understand thy commandments more fully every day and to live by them in sincere confidence. Preserve my heart so that I shall never again become forgetful and ungrateful, that I may never seek after other gods or other consolation on earth or in any creature, but cling truly and solely to thee, my only God. Amen, dear Lord God and Father. Amen."

Afterward, if time and inclination permit, the Second Commandment likewise in four strands, like this: "You shall not take the name of the Lord your God in vain," etc. First, I learn that I must keep God's name in honor, holiness, and beauty; not to swear, curse, not to be boastful or seek honor and repute for myself, but humbly to invoke his name, to pray, praise, and extol it, and to let it be my only honor and glory that he is my God and that I am his lowly creature and unworthy servant. Second, I give thanks to him for these precious gifts, that he has revealed his name to me and bestowed it upon me, that I can glory in his name and be called God's servant and creature, etc., that his name is my refuge like a mighty fortress to which the righteous man can flee and find protection, as Solomon says [Proverbs 18:10]. Third, I confess and acknowledge that I have grievously and shamefully sinned against this commandment all my life, I have not only failed to invoke, extol, and honor his holy name, but have also been ungrateful for such gifts and have, by swearing, lying, and betraying, misused them in the pursuit of shame and sin. This I bitterly regret and ask grace and forgiveness, etc. Fourth, I ask for help and strength henceforth to learn [to obey] this commandment and to be preserved from such evil ingratitude, abuse, and sin against his name, and that I may be found grateful in revering and honoring his name.

I repeat here what I previously said in reference to the Lord's Prayer: if in the midst of such thoughts the Holy Spirit begins to preach in your heart with rich, enlightening thoughts, honor him by letting go of this written scheme; be still and listen to him who can do better than you can.

Remember what he says and note it well and you will behold wondrous things in the law of God, as David says [Psalm 119:18].

The Third Commandment: "Remember the Sabbath day, to keep it holy." I learn from this, first of all, that the Sabbath day has not been instituted for the sake of being idle or indulging in worldly pleasures, but in order that we may keep it holy. However, it is not sanctified by our works and actions—our works are not holy—but by the word of God, which alone is wholly pure and sacred and which sanctifies everything that comes in contact with it, be it time, place, person, labor, rest, etc. According to St. Paul, who says that every creature is consecrated by word and prayer, 1 Timothy 4 [5], our works are consecrated through the word. I realize therefore that on the Sabbath I must, above all, hear and contemplate God's word. Thereafter I should give thanks in my own words, praise God for all his benefits, and pray for myself and for the whole world. He who so conducts himself on the Sabbath day keeps it holy. He who fails to do so is worse than the person who works on the Sabbath.

Second, I thank God in this commandment for his great and beautiful goodness and grace which he has given us in the preaching of his word. And he has instructed us to make use of it, especially on the Sabbath day, for the meditation of the human heart can never exhaust such a treasure. His word is the only light in the darkness of this life, a word of life, consolation, and supreme blessedness. Where this precious and saving word is absent, nothing remains but a fearsome and terrifying darkness, error and faction, death and every calamity, and the tyranny of the devil himself, as we can see with our own eyes every day.

Third, I confess and acknowledge great sin and wicked ingratitude on my part because all my life I have made disgraceful use of the Sabbath and have thereby despised his precious and dear word in a wretched way. I have been too lazy, listless, and uninterested to listen to it, let alone to have desired it sincerely or to have been grateful for it. I have let my dear God proclaim his word to me in vain, have dismissed the noble treasure, and have trampled it underfoot. He has tolerated this in his great and divine mercy and has not ceased in his fatherly, divine love and faithfulness to keep on preaching to me and calling me to the salvation of my soul. For this I repent and ask for grace and forgiveness.

Fourth, I pray for myself and for the whole world that the gracious Father may preserve us in his holy word and not withdraw it from us because of our sin, ingratitude, and laziness. May he preserve us from factious spirits and false teachers, and may he send faithful and honest laborers into his harvest [Matthew 9:38], that is, devout pastors and preachers. May he grant us grace humbly to hear, accept, and honor their words as his own words and to offer our sincere thanks and praise.

The Fourth Commandment: "Honor your father and your mother." First, I learn to acknowledge God, my Creator; how wondrously he has created me, body and soul; and how he has given me life through my parents and has instilled in them the desire to care for me, the fruit of their bodies, with all their power. He has brought me into this world, has sustained and cared for me, nurtured and educated me with great diligence, carefulness, and concern, through danger, trouble, and hard work. To this moment he protects me, his creature, and helps me in countless dangers and troubles. It is as though he were creating me anew every moment. But the devil does not willingly concede us one single moment of life.

Second, I thank the rich and gracious Creator on behalf of myself and all the world that he has established and assured in the commandment the increase and preservation of the human race, that is, of households and of states. Without these two institutions or governments the world could not exist a single year, because without government there can be no peace, and where there is no peace there can be no family; without family, children cannot be begotten or raised, and fatherhood and motherhood would cease to be. It is the purpose of this commandment to guard and preserve both family and state, to admonish children and subjects to be obedient, and to enforce it, too, and to let no violation go unpunished—otherwise children would have disrupted the family long ago by their disobedience, and subjects would have disorganized the state and laid it to waste for they outnumber parents and rulers. There are no words to fully describe the benefit of this commandment.

Third, I confess and lament my wicked disobedience and sin; in defiance of God's commandment I have not honored or obeyed my parents; I have often provoked and offended them, have been impatient with their parental discipline, have been resentful and scornful of their loving admonition and have rather gone along with loose company and evil companions. God himself condemns such disobedient children and withholds from them a long life; many of them succumb and perish in disgrace before they reach adulthood. Whoever does not obey father and mother must obey the executioner or otherwise come, through God's wrath, to an evil end, etc. Of all this I repent and ask for grace and forgiveness.

Fourth, I pray for myself and for all the world that God would bestow his grace and pour his blessing richly upon the family and the state. Grant that from this time on we may be devout, honor our parents, obey our superiors, and resist the devil when he entices us to be disobedient and rebellious, and so may we help improve home and nation by our actions and thus preserve the peace, all to the praise and glory of God for our own benefit and for the prosperity of all. Grant that we may acknowledge these his gifts and be thankful for them.

At this point we should add a prayer for our parents and superiors, that God may grant them understanding and wisdom to govern and rule us in peace and happiness. May he preserve them from tyranny, from riot and fury, and turn them to honor God's word and not oppress it, nor persecute anyone or do injustice. Such excellent gifts must be sought by prayer, as St. Paul teaches; otherwise the devil will reign in the palace and everything fall into chaos and confusion.

If you are a father or mother, you should at this point remember your children and the workers in your household. Pray earnestly to the dear Father, who has set you in an office of honor in his name and intends that you be honored by the name "father." Ask that he grant you grace and blessing to look after and support your wife, children, and servants in a godly and Christian manner. May he give you wisdom and strength to train them well in heart and will to follow your instruction with obedience. Both are God's gifts, your children and the way they flourish, that they turn out well and that they remain so. Otherwise the home is nothing but a pigsty and school for rascals, as one can see among the uncouth and godless.

The Fifth Commandment: "You shall not kill." Here I learn, first of all, that God desires me to love my neighbor, so that I do him no bodily harm, either by word or action, neither injure nor take revenge upon him in anger, vexation, envy, hatred, or for any evil reason, but realize that I am obliged to assist and counsel him in every bodily need. In this commandment God commands me to protect my neighbor's body and in turn commands my neighbor to protect my own. As Sirach says, "He has committed to each of us his neighbor" [Ecclesiasticus 9:14].

Second, I give thanks for such ineffable love, providence, and faithfulness toward me by which he has placed this mighty shield and wall to protect my physical safety. All are obliged to care for me and protect me, and I, in turn, must behave likewise toward others. He upholds this command and, where it is not observed, he has established the sword as punishment for those who do not live up to it. Were it not for this excellent commandment and ordinance, the devil would instigate such a massacre among men that no

The world does not know Me

The world is not the earth. The world is all that lives on earth, but does not lift itself to God, the Eternal. This world is the worldly one who views the planet earth as the only true and real, whose horizon rises only as far as the clouds. Beyond that all is deaf and dumb to him.

The one who has no eyes for Me does not see Me. The one who has no ears for Me does not hear Me. The one who has no refined sense of smell does not smell the fragrance which streams from the life, which I Am.

A person who craves only the delights of the world does not taste what the life offers him for daily consumption.

He reaches for animal products, for his sense of touch has not been refined either. It is not noble and does not touch beautiful and delicate things in the light and radiance of the Godhead.

My child, I love you. My child, great is the love I have for My children. No person can have even an inkling of My love who does not behold with his spiritual eyes the universe in all its radiance and in the manifold diversity of My life.

See, everything that exists is the expression of My love. All Being bears witness to an impersonal Creator-Spirit, which I Am.

See, My child, every movement of your body, each breath, everything that you feel and speak bears witness to a mighty, eternal, omnipresent power.

Even the child who slanders Me, who takes My name in vain, who does violence to the life, see, My power is in everything, in everyone and in all things. I give it to My child, to each individual in the same way. This is the impersonal love, the impersonal life.

See, from this you can sense how great My love is. I do not strike back; I do not punish; I give Myself in each person, in each soul, in all Being.

Just as the sun does not ask the human children: Is how I am shining pleasant to you? Or: Is it okay with you that I shine?

45

See, My child, the sun gives and gives; it follows its course indefatigably. The sun gives and gives to the moon and the stars, which in turn give to the earth and the human beings. The whole solar system gives, including the earth. The earth gives. See, from this you recognize in a small way the great, universal Giver, the spirit of love.

My child, the hearts of My children which beat for Me in the right way are receiving My love increasingly more. For they turn their hearts to Me, just as the calyx of a flower gives itself to the sunlight, so that it can absorb the sun's rays deeply into itself.

Oh recognize My impersonal love! The more My child surrenders to Me, the impersonal life, and becomes itself impersonal, the more it will receive from this impersonal power, from My love, until it becomes itself the love, My image, self-luminous, radiating for all people and beings, for all Being. My child, this is love: I Am, and you, too, may be.

Become impersonal

Personalistic thinking, thinking that re-
volves around one's own person, is human. The more a person thinks about
himself, about his welfare, the more
limited his consciousness will become.
The one who thinks only of himself is
still far away from Me, the impersonal.

I Am the impersonal life, the fullness. I
Am who I Am in everything, also in
you, My child.

I Am the fullness. I Am everything; be
aware of this! The fullness, everything
that exists, Am I, and I Am in you. Are
you aware of this? If so, then why are
you afraid of people and things which
are outside of your higher self? With

this anxiety you lend the power to people and things to dominate you.

The one who has soared into an impersonal life stands above all human emotions and inclinations; he is impersonal. He no longer thinks about himself, whether this or that would be good for him. He knows that he has everything; for the fullness, I, the impersonal, dwell in the center of his soul and in each cell of his body.

Many of My children worry about the coming time. Therefore, in this time they only have that to which they are oriented—or much less, depending on how much doubt and fear they bring into their planning for the coming time. And so, My child, the person who clings to personalistic thinking is limiting himself by striving to possess everything possible, to provide for every eventuality that may take place in the coming time at all.

Free yourself from this! Act at all times in accordance with the Spirit! If you know that you will depart from the temporal tomorrow, then plant a tree today for those who will remain behind, but only if you have an inner urge to do so. This is impersonal thinking and acting in the spirit of impersonal love, which sets one free.

The one who does not think of himself, who gives only out of the inner fullness: light, strength, love and good will, verily, he will have the fullness at all times and in all eternity.

Eternity is your goal

You are a child of eternity. Be aware of this!

There is no interruption to life, for everything is life. In all of infinity there is no standstill, and so not in you, in your life, either.

Dead is only the person and soul which focused all striving and aspirations on the outer world, on matter. The heart of the soul will one day return to that place where its treasure is, to matter, to which it paid homage as a human being, and whose delights and vices it considered to be its true self.

Just as constricted as the human consciousness was, so will the soul live in a similar way. Though it is a child of eternity, of infinity, it will tie itself to time and space and will lavish care and attention on these deranged thoughts, that it is a child of this world, a child of matter.

Let your consciousness soar to all the spiritual universes from Order to Mercy; link with the universal Spirit that is everything in all things. This awakens in you the thinking in terms of eternity, the awareness that experiences only unending beauty and purity, and that is one with all life.

The beauty of the soul

The beauty of the soul is its purity.
You attain this beauty through a noble
disposition and selfless, lofty thoughts.
The more selfless you become and the
nobler your thoughts and your basic
attitude are, the more beautiful your
soul will become.

Only beauty and nobility can flow
from a beautiful, pure soul. And out of
a soul filled with selfless love, only
love can, in turn, stream forth. From a
heart and a soul filled with My peace,
only peace can flow. And out of a har-
monious person, only harmony can
flow, because through the love which
dwells in him he is filled only with
harmony.

All that is in you finds expression in your nature; it marks your type and behavior.

How do you find inner beauty, purity, love and harmony?

Be aware that I, the spirit of life, dwell in you.

I Am everything in all things. I Am who I Am, the life. See everything that you behold with your inner eyes, with the eyes of the soul.

See, when you are aware that I Am the love, harmony and peace in all things, and when you meet with love everything that is, nothing contrary can happen to you. The pure and noble life will connect with your pure, noble and selfless thoughts and give you more than you can imagine.

My child, trillionfold life streams toward you from all Being. That Am I, who loves you.

Constantly keep in touch with Me, by day and by night. Then I Am consciously in you and you are consciously in Me.

Let love stream from your being, then you are truly a child of blessing for this world and for all Being; then you will one day enter radiantly into My life, into eternity.

Eternity

The eternity, the life, is hidden in all Being.

Let your consciousness reach out to the nature kingdoms, to the heavenly bodies, to people, souls, beings and animals. Let your consciousness flow; let it flow toward the core of being which is contained in all Being.

Just as the bee goes deeply into the calyx of a flower, so let your consciousness enter deeply into all Being. Do not be content with the shell, with matter. If you are satisfied merely with the husk, you will experience the limitation of time and space again and again, because you look at the physical with physical eyes.

Let your inner being, your awakened feelings, your consciousness, stream forth deeply into the nature kingdoms, into the heavenly bodies, into all Being.

Then the core of being of life, which I Am, will open up to you. You will then behold eternity, spaceless and timeless life, and you will feel at one with Me. Then fear and worry will recede; death no longer has a shadow, because you have penetrated matter.

Death

Death is limited thinking. Death is earthly, constricted awareness.

The one who lives in the face of death
is already spiritually dead. He thinks
that he lives, but he does not live. His
life is simply a vegetating away, a state
of languishing infirmity which does
not end, but starts anew in death: vegetating away as a soul, reincarnating,
vegetating away, infirmity and death.
This will be the fate of both soul and
person, until soul and person awaken
and walk the path of self-recognition.

Self-recognition sets you free

Acknowledge yourself as My child; become independent from yourself and from all people, and you will become free.

A person cannot do anything of himself. What he possesses, what he acquires, that Am I.

See, I give Myself. I Am everything in all things, also in your neighbor. I also give Myself to you through people who love you and who have taken on the task to provide for you in this life.

And so, never demand goods or money from anyone. Accept thankfully whatever you receive and see Me as the Giver in this.

Do not waste what you receive. Observe moderation in all things and with everything, for what has been given to you through second or third persons is from Me.

I serve you through your neighbor, through the sun, moon and stars; I serve you through the nature kingdoms. Accept thankfully whatever you receive, for all that is good and of love comes from Me.

I care for you day and night. I watch over you, My child, for I, your Father, love you.

See, My child, the one who entrusts himself to Me receives. Do not take anything that you receive as a matter of course. And whatever you possess, administer it well. See yourself only as a child that has been richly blessed with gifts! But do not hoard My gifts.

I care; I give; I help; I heal. Recognize Me in everything and accept everything thankfully, even if for the moment it seems to be filled with suffering. Know that many a soul matures through suffering.

Actualize My law, which is everything, then you will truly receive from the fullness. The one who is greedy for My gifts, who grabs My gifts for himself, considering them to be his property, holds on to them and says: "Me, me, me, only me, everything for me!" This child will lose everything one day and will stand before Me as a beggar.

See, that is bondage, that is being bound and the imprisonment of the soul. Those who live in egotism, who think only of themselves, who defend My gifts and want to possess even more of them, will become impoverished according to the law of cause and effect. They will lose everything; everything will be taken from them through the law of sowing and reaping.

Someday, each soul must recognize its own self; its nakedness and exposure, its small ego that wants to shine and which must be sacrificed in order to become truly free in Me, the free God, the eternal Giver, who is everything in all things.

The selfless sacrifice

Do not defend yourself and do not defend anything that has been given to you to simply have and administer.

The one who defends himself and My gifts is bound. A bound person cannot free himself, unless he sacrifices himself to Me, the Eternal.

My child, sacrifice yourself through My love. See, love is the strongest power in the universe; this love is always giving and sacrificing.

Whatever you do should be imbued by selfless love. This is possible only if you do not look to the flesh but rather to the core of being of each soul.

See through matter and connect with the core of being, with Me, the Godhead. Then you will behold only purity; you will see only love and can give only love, because purity and love will communicate with your selfless heart, and you will live impersonally according to the law.

Become impersonal!

Egocentric thinking

Personalistic thinking is human, ego-centric thinking. It is constricting and self-centered. It is thinking in terms of space and time and is a way of thinking that is not free.

Such thinking makes a person small and petty. It leads to hatred and enmity and this, in turn, to theft and binding, because the limited ego-thinker only wants to own everything for himself that is worth striving for.

This selfish heart is far from Me, because it wants only to receive and not to give. This person is not a free child of true life, but a worldly person, focused on matter, which ultimately is nothing more than My transformed-down spirit, transformed-down consciousness, and, in the end, My possession.

But I am not concerned about My possession. Whatever is Mine is also yours; and what belongs to Me belongs to you, too.

The one who administers his property, which is also My property, in the right way, in the awareness that all is spirit and shall be, in turn, lifted up to the highest principle, will recognize Me, the Giver, in everything, thus becoming impersonal and acting accordingly. He will no longer think of himself, but of Me, the One who is everything in all things.

My child, only then can you truly receive and become free from your self, from your personalistic thinking.

Become free of your self

Build on God; trust Me under all situations in life; be impersonal! Do not demand anything for yourself, give! One day every human being will have to let go of everything in order to become free for the true journey of the soul to the light of the Godhead.

For this reason, become free! Do not tie yourself to any person; instead feel linked with each person as a unit in the filiation of God.

Become free of your self-will and practice recognizing My will. You will soon recognize My will if you test yourself: Is your thinking still willful? Do you want, or do you give yourself to Me, the One who directs all things?

Examine your words! How often do you still talk about yourself? From this, too, you can recognize your self-will, your egocentricity. Examine yourself, how often, when, and why you defend yourself. From this, too, you recognize your ego and your self-will.

Become impersonal; become radiant! Give love and light, and you will stand in the light of your Father.

Stand in Me, in My light

You shall be the reflection of My life.

Whatever you do, think about it. Ask yourself if Jesus of Nazareth would have acted as you would like to act. Place your thoughts, your words and your actions into the light of the Nazarene and recognize yourself in them as My child.

Give light through selflessness and it will become light in and around you.

I Am the light. In My light nothing remains hidden. Everything will be revealed; My light will reflect everything, your good as well as your base thoughts, words and deeds. The light is the power of the seed, for without light nothing can flourish. Therefore, My light will germinate your seed, make it sprout and grow, until you recognize yourself in your own fruit, and then weed out the bad seed along with its taproot by the way of self-conquest.

Then it will become lighter and brighter in you and you will sow good seeds and reap good fruit. See, I take only good fruit back into the light, into My light. I do not hide the light of My child under the bushel; I place it on top of the bushel so that it gives light to many.

My child, so shine and radiate, become selfless and forget yourself, then the universe will serve you and all those who inhabit it in pure light garments.

Let your thoughts be the same as your words

My child, if it is possible for you to express all that you think, and if your words are the same as your thoughts, if they are the heavenly music of the spheres, melodies of love which do not enchant the hearts, but wake them up and make them listen, then you live freely.

If your thoughts and words are lawful, then you will accomplish truly heroic deeds in My spirit.

See, small and often trivial are the deeds of those who render lip-service to Me but do not carry Me in their hearts. These deeds of pretence, which are based only on self-love and to show oneself off, are as sound and fury before Me, the Absolute.

See, I have created perfect children. I cannot be active in those who do not strive for perfection in thoughts, words and deeds.

Be heroic, willing to make sacrifices! Sacrifice yourself, your human ego, your personalistic thinking, your opinions, your desires, your base inclinations and yearnings, your personalistic striving.

Become impersonal! Conscious, selfless life is God's life.

Live consciously

Whatever you do, do it totally and check your actions, whether they can be endorsed by Me, the Christ.

Turn away from the stimulation of the senses and sensual desires; strive for the higher love; then you will climb toward God's love and you will link with the absolute love, with Me, My child.

The high love is the mystical love. It is the mystical giving which enables you to grow and to mature in the knowledge that the love, too, has its levels from Order to Mercy.

Once you have climbed to the seventh level, you have walked through all degrees of love and have worked your way up to the absolute love, to the unification with Me, the absolute love. Then you are truly one with Me, and you experience a high time of joy and happiness which you have been able to enjoy only partially on your path through all the levels to the absolute love.

Now you truly rest in the arms of your bridegroom who draws you to His bosom both as bride and child, and who gives you the blissful kiss which weds you to Him, the great All-One, to whom you then belong for all eternity.

Become My bride

I Am your bridegroom; come, My bride, adorn yourself with the garland of virtue, with the scepter of peace, with the heroic striving to please Me completely.

Gird yourself with selfless love and ennoble yourself in all things! Dissociate yourself from all the compulsive drives. May your striving know only one aim: purity, purity at all cost.

Exchange self-will for God's will; exchange self-love for childlike love! Surrender your base inclinations for high and noble feelings! Sacrifice your sensual inclinations and become of like mind with Me!

My only aspiration is to unite with you, I, the purity and love itself. If this is also your striving, then you will vibrate more highly each day and you will draw closer to Me, the One who I Am from eternity to eternity.

Walk on the path of virtue and meekness. Sacrifice your passions, your egotistic thoughts; then you will hear your lofty bridegroom and you will feel, think, speak and act as He wants you to. Yes, your speech and your actions will be the same as the I Am, your bridegroom. Come, My bride!

You are truly My beloved

Beloved child, listen to Me, your Father and Lord, and do as I advise you.

See, the more you live in the spirit of your Father, the closer you come to Me.

Many a child of Mine believes that I favor certain of My human children on this earth. Such thinking is human and not spiritual. The spirit of life favors none of His children. The difference lies in the fact that one child has grown closer to My love-streaming heart than another.

See, people in southern lands, where it is warmer than in the north, would never say they are more loved by the sun than people in the north. It is the universal law which, according to its intensity, has a different effect in the southern lands than in the northern ones. However, the sun shines equally at all times.

When you are closer to the heart of your Father through your longing and your spiritual striving for Me, then you will feel the warming and enveloping rays of My heart of love more than a child which is still standing in the shadow of its feelings and passions.

Despite everything, the spirit of love does speak to His child which is still entangled in egotism: My beloved child, come away from your limitations, burst open the armor of the human ego, so that the eternal light can shine upon you and set you free from all that is human, so that you truly live through Me, the I Am from eternity to eternity.

I Am

Awaken in Me daily more; I Am in all Being. Behold nature in Me, the I Am. Nature lives because I Am.

Behold the stone, the minerals, with your spiritual eyes. Let the primordial sensation stream from your inner being, then it will ring consciously in your inner ear: I Am the power in the stone; I Am the life.

Behold the flowers and shrubs, the trees and fruit with your inner eyes. Communicate with the inner forces that are active in all things and again you will hear Me, the breath of your heavenly Father, who whispers to you: My child, I Am.

I Am the sun; I Am every heavenly body. I Am the firmament and all Being. I Am the nature; I Am the stone, the mineral, the flower, the shrub, the fruit.

I Am.

I Am in every little animal; I Am its life. Do not extinguish it wantonly, rather look upon it as your second neighbor. Give to it from your selfless love, for I Am the power in the animal, too, the love and the radiance of, the sun.

Love, love, My child! Smother with love all that is low and evil. In particular, love your neighbor, your sister and brother. See, I Am also the power in each one of you, the Father-Mother-

Spirit, the love that wants to lead and guide the child.

Live consciously, My child, and fulfill the holy laws, then your soul will soon tune in again to the inner jubilation and the stream of the holy primordial sensation will totally vivify you.

Then you will speak consciously and feel consciously, in the deep recognition that the Father and I are one.

Only in this way, can you and will you love Me more than this world.

Be free from yourself

To be free from oneself means to think less and less about oneself and one's own affairs.

To be free means not to strive for property and goods, but to entrust oneself to the One who knows about all things, who is everything.

The one who is truly free is rich. And the one who is rich in his inner being does not strive for possessions. He has everything, and everything serves him.

This freedom cannot be acquired with wealth and goods, but only with a heart of gold, which does not think about itself but beats only for its neighbor.

People with golden hearts are truly happy. They are the movers of the world who bring peace to this world by being selfless and by forgetting themselves.

Become free, My child, from personalistic thinking, from personal feeling and wanting, then you will receive what you need for your life and more.

Walk over green, fragrant pastures; they are yours. Walk over flowering meadows, through rustling woods; they are yours. All that you behold bears in itself the eternal Spirit, your heritage. It is yours, because the substance of all life is in you.

Learn to make use of your heritage in the right way, and infinity will serve you.

Infinity, the spirit in all Being, serves you

Everything that is wants to serve you, the universal child, the highest life which has taken on form.

See, My child, what you see is consciousness. The consciousness of an individual universal life has been created by Me in such a way that it serves the higher consciousness.

You, as the second-highest consciousness, as a child of God, have the gift to make the entire universal life serve you.

Subdue the earth, I once said to My own. With this I meant: When man learns to correctly recognize and interpret the aspects of consciousness of the earth, then he will begin to sense what universal consciousness is, the Holy Spirit in all Being.

My child, refine your senses, make room in your inner being for all realms of consciousness and you will learn that you are truly the highest creature after Me, your Father, for infinity, the all-consciousness, My spirit, serves you.

Spirit is consciousness; spirit is power. I Am everything in all things, the spirit of your Father, the servant of all His children.

Attain this high consciousness by giving through the Giver. Give, as I give

Myself eternally, I, the Spirit, the power of your Father.

I Am the Eternal, the eternal Giver.

To give makes one free

My child, you have everything that I have. Recognize and grasp this statement in its depth.

The one who has everything that infinity has to offer, what else could he possibly want? Enter into your heritage by believing and trusting in Me, then your love for Me will also grow and flourish.

Recognize: Nothing happens by chance in all of infinity. Everything is well-ordered and integrated into My great law. Strive to come away from the law of cause and effect, of sowing and reaping, then you will truly experience your heritage and you can use it in the right way.

one could live in safety for a single hour—as happens when God becomes angry and inflicts punishment upon a disobedient and ungrateful world.

Third, I confess and lament my own wickedness and that of the world, not only that we are so terribly ungrateful for such fatherly love and solicitude toward us—but what is especially scandalous, that we do not acknowledge this commandment and teaching, are unwilling to learn it, and neglect it as though it did not concern us or we had no part in it. We amble along complacently, feel no remorse that in defiance of this commandment we neglect our neighbor, and, yes, we desert him, persecute, injure, or even kill him in our thoughts. We indulge in anger, rage, and villainy as though we were doing a fine and noble thing. Really, it is high time that we started to deplore and bewail how much we have acted like rogues and like unseeing, unruly, and unfeeling persons who kick, scratch, tear, and devour one another like furious beasts and pay no heed to this serious and divine command, etc.

Fourth, I pray the dear Father to lead us to an understanding of this his sacred commandment and to help us keep it and live in accordance with it. May he preserve us from the murderer who is the master of every form of murder and violence. May he grant us his grace that we and all others may treat each other in kindly, gentle, charitable ways, forgiving one another from the heart, bearing each other's faults and shortcomings in a Christian and brotherly manner and thus living together in true peace and concord, as the commandment teaches and requires us to do.

The Sixth Commandment: "You shall not commit adultery." Here I learn once more what God intends and expects me to do, namely, to live chastely, decently, and temperately, both in thoughts and in words and actions, and not to disgrace any man's wife,

How small and lowly are those who are poor in spirituality! They hoard and dispute; they quarrel and complain, and yet they are poor and remain poor until they recognize their true heritage, which can be gained only through the right humility and selflessness.

My child, accept everything as it is and do not complain! Everything that happens to you, joy and sorrow, is you, yourself. You are the builder of your fate, but you are also the conqueror of your true, eternal heritage.

Just as you behave, so are you. Just as you make your bed today—so will you sleep on it tomorrow. Realize this, My child.

See all these things in the light of mercy and love. These attributes of your Father show all your still existing human inclinations and drives, so that you sacrifice them to Me, the Eternal, on the altar of mercy and love.

True sacrifice liberates; it leads to the right deed. Sacrifice your ego and enter into your true eternal heritage, the universal life, which I Am; then infinity, the life, will serve you.

I Am the life.

Sacrifice

To sacrifice oneself on My altar of love is the most difficult thing for My human children. In order to give up all worldly things, to gain the great whole, one needs inner greatness and trust in God.

The one who sacrifices himself initially sees nothing but smoke, the smoke of his passions and drives, of his vain thoughts and longings.

Once the smoke has lifted, then the one striving toward God initially sees nothing but ashes, the ashes of his own base ego.

Now he needs to search in the ashes for a sliver of glowing ember, the

Christ-light. This means again working on yourself, My child.

The one who wants to sacrifice himself to Me must now remove the ashes of his still existing base ego and must fan the Christ-light, the smoldering sliver of ember of his soul, with the belief that through the Christ-light he will grow nearer to Me, God, the Eternal.

This means more sacrifices. Daily, by the hour, and every minute, he must watch himself, watch his ever recurring low thoughts, which rise anew, again and again, in the human mind and want to cover up the Christ-light.

With heroic sacrificial courage, he must fight against the layers covering the soul, the still existing soul garments, the subconscious and the consciousness, until the entire root system of the human ego is removed from the field of the soul, and the brain cells register only what is noble, pure and beautiful, and the senses feel and desire only what is noble.

Recognize this, My child: Then you will truly intensify the Christ-light in you, which will then unite with the primordial light of your Father.

Get going on the work of great deeds! Begin! Sacrifice yourself and cleanse everything which still clings to you as humanness; then through trust and belief, you will find your way to the true love and the unification with Me, your God and Father.

Clear up all that moves you

My child, you possess several aspects of will. These are the consciousness, the subconscious and the soul garments. These aspects form the human will, the self-centered feeling, thinking and wanting.

See, My child, if you want to become free of yourself, of your base ego, then do not put off the problems that move you over and over again. Overcome them with the spiritual effort of will by surrendering to Me all that has not yet been conquered.

Again and again, place it on My altar of love until you are free from the problem you are struggling with. No matter how often it seems to overwhelm you, place it in good time on My altar of love. I, your Father, will transform that part which you leave on My altar.

Keep bringing to Me those parts of your problems which, despite your sacrificial efforts, always lend you wings and keep urging you, until everything has been transformed by Me, your Lord and God, your Father.

See, My child, the human being will be engaged in a struggle until all has been conquered by the power of My Son, the Christ-Redeemer-Power; until he has freed himself of his self-centered feeling, thinking and wanting; until the consciousness and subconscious have become thoroughly spiritualized and the soul garments have become filled with light.

See, My child, these things must be overcome by soul and person alone, yet with the supporting and helping flame of the Redeemer, with Christ, My Son. Come, get going. Begin!

Walk with Me;
I Am your companion

Wherever you go or are, you are in the garden of love when I, the spirit of life, am your companion.

Walk in the awareness of God, that I Am everything in all things; then the nature kingdoms will bow before you, My child, and from the thorny bushes that perhaps edge your path, spiritual roses will grow in honor of the One who consciously goes with you and in your honor, for you are My image.

Behold everything in My consciousness. Let your consciousness flow into the minerals, into the plants and the animals and feel the unity with all forms of life, then you will realize that the essence of your being is present in all forms of life and the essence of all forms of life is in you.

See, My child, if you violate an animal, your consciousness suffers and in time you will suffer, too, because you have burdened yourself by maltreating the animal, and thus have done damage to yourself.

Realize that whosoever violates nature, whosoever consciously causes animals to suffer, will one day suffer himself, because he has violated himself and has brought suffering upon himself, because a part of his consciousness is in all life forms; the essence of all forms of life is in him, in the soul of the person.

Understand this and act accordingly! Then I shall become your conscious companion and we shall walk hand in hand through the garden of infinity, knowing, My child, that what is Mine is also yours, and what is yours, that Am I, your companion. I give you a rose from the heavens, it is you, yourself, My pure child. I Am the core of being and you are the jewel of the inner life, the garment of love.

I Am love

My love is boundless. It knows neither time nor space. All that exists is the expression of My love.

Even the evil which finds expression in this world bears My love within itself. See, the evil could never forgive if it were entirely evil. In evil there lies the predisposition for the good; in it lies the transforming and forgiving principle, the love. Through love alone will man find his way to forgiveness and only through love will he be forgiven.

Recognize the greatness in the almighty, all-effective power of God, your Father!

The evil, the bad and the satanic, are never only evil, bad and satanic, no matter to what degree the baseness finds expression and rages.

In everything, in the noble and the good as well as in the bad, the bestial, is love the maintaining and transforming principle. And so, I Am the All-Spirit which is present in all things and which in the end leads everything to the good, pure and noble, to Me, the love, whose expression I Am.

Become one who beholds

In everything I Am the universal spirit of life. Recognize Me first in yourself, and strive for perfection, so that you will again become divine as I have created you. If you lift your thoughts and longings to Me, the Eternal, then you will recognize and behold Me, the life, in everything.

The vision for eternal things is closed for the man of the world; for the spiritual person much is apparent; he beholds Me, the essence of life, in all Being.

Once you recognize the essence of all Being in yourself, then you will behold yourself as a part of the universe and will recognize yourself in all things.

Recognize and experience in yourself that I Am all that is noble, good and pure, for I Am the life. There is no life except Me. I Am everything in all things. Thus, your life, too, is the life in all things, because I Am in you and you are in Me.

Recognize yourself as part of the great totality which again bears in itself all parts of life. And so, you are universal life from Me. Because everything is contained in all things, so are you, as essence of life, also in everything.

Behold Me in you, and you behold Me in all forms of life.

If you harm your neighbor, you harm yourself, because as the essence of life, you, too, are in your neighbor. If you slander and mock your neighbor, or rob and reject him, then you slander and mock yourself and at the same time Me, since I Am in all things, as well as being the essence of your life. If you rob and reject your neighbor, you rob yourself of your life force and you reject your true self and at the same time Me, who is the I Am in all things.

If you violate the plant and animal kingdoms, you violate yourself; you sink to the level of the bestial, thus reducing your life force which I Am. Realize this and behold the life in all things; then you behold Me.

The truly wise one beholds people and beings, all Being, in the light of the Godhead. This is why, he is illuminated and wise, since he simultaneously senses what life is, the law. I Am the law in you, I, your Lord and God from eternity to eternity.

Be conscious of the great whole, for you are universal life, since I Am in you and you are in Me, the life.

What you think is what you are

The expression of your outer form, your gestures and facial expressions, your clothing and your conduct portray your thoughts. The one who beholds you knows who you are; the one who merely sees you does not recognize you.

For this reason, learn to recognize yourself; then you will also learn to behold. Then you will behold people and things with the eyes of the Spirit, to whom all things are manifest. As long as you still merely see, you look only at the outer form. You pass judgement on the outer; you judge because you do not recognize yourself.

daughter, or maidservant. More than this, I ought to assist, save, protect, and guard marriage and decency to the best of my ability; I should silence the idle thoughts of those who want to destroy and slander their reputation. All this I am obliged to do, and God expects me not only to leave my neighbor's wife and family unmolested, but I owe it to my neighbor to preserve and protect his good character and honor, just as I would want my neighbor to do for me and mine in keeping with this commandment.

Second, I thank my faithful and dear Father for his grace and benevolence by which he accepts my husband, son, servant, wife, daughter, maidservant into his care and protection and forbids so sternly and firmly anything that would bring them into disrepute. He protects and upholds this commandment and does not leave violations unpunished, even though he himself has to act if someone disregards and violates the commandment and precept. No one escapes him; he must either pay the penalty or eventually atone for such lust in the fires of hell. God desires chastity and will not tolerate adultery. That can be seen every day when the impenitent and profligate are overtaken by the wrath of God and perish miserably. Otherwise it would be impossible to guard one's wife, child, and servants against the devil's filthiness for a single hour or preserve them in honor and decency. What would happen would be unbridled immorality and beastliness, as happens when God in his wrath withdraws his hand and permits everything to go to wrack and ruin.

Third, I confess and acknowledge my sin, my own and that of all the world, how I have sinned against this commandment my whole life in thought, word, and action. Not only have I been ungrateful for these excellent teachings and gifts, but I have complained and rebelled against the divine requirement

The one who passes sentence and makes judgements can be certain that something similar can be found in himself. The one who writes off his neighbor has in himself what he condemns in his neighbor or maliciously attributes to him.

Recognize yourself in your neighbor. How you think about him, what you think of him, this is your own self. But the one who beholds has explored himself and beholds people and things with the inner eyes of mercy, with the expression of understanding, of good will, of understanding love.

Become a beholder!

"The Father and I are one"

These words by Jesus are words of Christ.

"The Father and I are one" means: *one* spirit, *one* life, *one* truth and *one* love.

See, child, one day each soul will find this oneness with Me through My eternal grace. Practice so that your thinking, feeling, willing and acting may become like Me, then you will reach the one stream which knows about all things, which beholds all things, which is all Being, God.

Become divine, become impersonal. Forget yourself; then you will gain Me, the impersonal One.

Think less and less of your small ego; instead let yourself be guided by Me, then you will gain Me. Do not interrupt when others are speaking; be quiet, be impersonal. Remain linked with Me, then I, the eternal power, will become active in you and your words will become weighty and mighty for all those who talk much of insignificant things. Be free of yourself, then your word will become My word.

Books from the Universal Life Series

This Is My Word
A and Ω
The Gospel of Jesus
The Christ-Revelation
which the world does not know
1078 pages / Order No. S 007en

The Sermon on the Mount
Life in accordance with the law of God
(an excerpt from "This Is My Word")
117 pages / Order No. S 008en

The INNER PATH, Collective Volume
The Original Christian School of Life
The Inner Path to Becoming One
with the Spirit of God In Us
7 books in one / 1344 pages / Order No. S150en

The Great Cosmic Teachings of
JESUS of Nazareth
to His Apostles and Disciples
Who Could Understand Them.
With explanations by Gabriele in the Great
Teaching Church of the Spirit of God
(Vol. 1) 255 pages / Order No. S 317en

For Parents and Children

Your Child and You
100 pages / Order No. S 110en

Luvy, the Bull
48 pages / Color illustrations / Order No. S 605en

The Cuckoo "Yoo-Hoo"
55 pages / Color illustrations / Order No. S 606en

Ten Little Black Boys
*A story to think about
and learn from, given from the light*
73 pages / Color illustrations / Order No. S 610en

For a free catalog of all our books,
cassettes and videos,
please contact:

Universal Life
The Inner Religion
P0 Box 3549
Woodbridge, CT 06525, U S A
Tel. 203-458-7771 • Fax 203-458-0713
1-800-846-2691

Verlag DAS WORT GmbH
im Universellen Leben
Max-Braun-Strasse 2
97828 Marktheidenfeld/Altfeld, Germany
Tel. 9391-504-132 • Fax 9391-504-133

E-mail: info@universelles-leben.org
Website: http://www.universelles-leben.org

of such decency and chastity, that God has not permitted all sorts of fornication and rascality to go unchecked and unpunished. He will not allow marriage to be despised, ridiculed, or condemned, etc. Sins against this commandment are, above all others, the grossest and most conspicuous and cannot be covered up or whitewashed. For this I am sorry, etc.

Fourth, I pray for myself and all the world that God may grant us grace to keep this commandment gladly and cheerfully in order that we might ourselves live in chastity and also help and support others to do likewise.

Then I continue with the other commandments as I have time or opportunity or am in the mood for it. As I have said before, I do not want anyone to feel bound by my words or thoughts. I only want to offer an example for those who may wish to follow it; let anyone improve it who is able to do so and let him meditate either upon all commandments at one time or on as many as he may desire. For the mind, once it is seriously occupied with a matter, be it good or evil, can ponder more in one moment than the tongue can recite in ten hours or the pen write in ten days. There is something quick, subtle, and mighty about the mind and soul. It is able to review the Ten Commandments in their fourfold aspect very rapidly if it wants to do so and is in earnest.

The Seventh Commandment: "You shall not steal." First, I can learn here that I must not take my neighbor's property from him or possess it against his will, either in secret or openly. I must not be false or dishonest in business, service, or work, nor profit by fraud, but must support myself by the sweat of my brow[10] and eat my bread in honor. Furthermore, I must see to it that in any of the above-named ways my neighbor is not defrauded, just as I wish for myself. I also learn in this commandment that God, in his fatherly solicitude, sets a protective hedge around my goods and solemnly prohibits anyone to steal from me. Where that is ignored, he has imposed a penalty and has placed the gallows and the rope in the hands of Jack the hangman. Where that cannot be done, God himself metes out punishment and they become beggars in the end, as the proverb says, "Who steals in his youth, goes begging in old age,"[11] or, "Stolen gain goes down the drain."[12]

In addition I give thanks for his steadfast goodness in that he has given such excellent teachings, assurance, and protection to me and to all the world. If it were not for his protection, not a penny or a crumb of bread would be left in the house.

Third, I confess my sins and ingratitude in such instances where I have wronged, deprived, or cheated anyone in my life.

Fourth, I ask that he grant to me and all the world grace to learn from this commandment, to ponder it, and to become better people, so that there may be less theft, robbery, usury, cheating, and injustice and that the Judgment Day, for which all saints and the whole creation pray, Romans 8 [20–23], shall soon bring this to an end. Amen.

The Eighth Commandment: "You shall not bear false witness." This teaches us, first of all, to be truthful to each other, to shun lies and calumnies, to be glad to speak well of each other, and to delight in hearing what is good about others. Thus a wall has been built around our good reputation and integrity to protect it against malicious gossip and deceitful tongues; God will not let that go unpunished, as he has said in the other commandments.

We owe him thanks both for the teachings and the protection which he has graciously provided for us.

Third, we confess and ask forgiveness that we have spent our lives in ingratitude and sin and have maligned our neighbor with false and wicked talk, though we owe him the same preservation of honor and integrity which we desire for ourselves.

Fourth, we ask for help from now on to keep the commandment and for a healing tongue, etc.

The Ninth and Tenth Commandments: "You shall not covet your neighbor's house." Similarly, "his wife," etc.

This teaches us first that we shall not dispossess our neighbor of his goods under pretense of legal claims, or lure away, alienate, or extort what is his, but help him to keep what is his, just as we wish to be done for ourselves. It is also a protection against the subtleties and chicaneries of shrewd manipulators who will receive their punishment in the end. Second, we should render thanks to him. Third, we should repentantly and sorrowfully confess our sins. Fourth, we should ask for help and strength devoutly to keep such divine commandments.[13]

These are the Ten Commandments in their fourfold aspect, namely, as a school text, song book, penitential book, and prayer book. They are intended to help the heart come to itself and grow zealous in prayer. Take care, however, not to undertake all of this or so much that one becomes weary in spirit. Likewise, a good prayer should not be lengthy or drawn out, but frequent and ardent. It is enough to consider one section or half a section which kindles a fire in the heart.[14] This the Spirit will grant us and continually instruct us in when, by God's word, our hearts have been cleared and freed of outside thoughts and concerns.

Nothing can be said here about the part of faith and Holy Scriptures [in prayer] because there would be no end to what could be said. With practice one can take the Ten Commandments on one day, a psalm or chapter of Holy Scripture the next day, and use them as flint and steel to kindle a flame in the heart.

A Simple Exercise
for Contemplating the Creed

If you have more time, or the inclination, you may treat the Creed in the same manner and make it into a garland of four strands. The Creed, however, consists of three main parts or articles, corresponding to the three Persons of the Divine Majesty, as it has been so divided in the Catechism and elsewhere.

The First Article of Creation

"I believe in God the Father Almighty, maker of heaven and earth."

Here, first of all, a great light shines into your heart if you permit it to and teaches you in a few words what all the languages of the world and a multitude of books cannot describe or fathom in words, namely, who you are, whence you came, whence came heaven and earth. You are God's creation, his handiwork, his workmanship. That is, of yourself and in yourself you are nothing, can do nothing, know nothing, are capable of nothing. What were you a thousand years ago? What were heaven and earth six thousand years ago? Nothing, just as that which will never be created is nothing. But what you are, know, can do, and can achieve is God's creation, as you confess [in the Creed] by word of mouth. Therefore you have nothing to boast of before God except that you are nothing and he is your Creator who can annihilate you at any moment. Reason knows nothing of such a light. Many great people have sought to know what heaven and earth, man and creatures are and have found no answer. But here it is declared and faith affirms that God has created everything out of nothing. Here is the soul's garden of pleasure, along whose paths we enjoy the works of God—but it would take too long to describe all that.

Furthermore, we should give thanks to God that in his kindness he has created us out of nothing and provides for our daily needs out of nothing—has made us to be such excellent beings with body and soul, intelligence, five senses, and has ordained us to be masters of earth, of fish, bird, and beast, etc. Here consider Genesis, chapters one to three.

Third, we should confess and lament our lack of faith and gratitude in failing to take this to heart, or to believe, ponder, and acknowledge it, and having been more stupid than unthinking beasts.

Fourth, we pray for a true and confident faith that sincerely esteems and trusts God to be our Creator, as this article declares.

The Second Article of Redemption

"And in Jesus Christ, his only Son, our Lord," etc.

Again a great light shines forth and teaches us how Christ, God's Son, has redeemed us from death which, after the creation, had become our lot through Adam's fall and in which we would have perished eternally. Now think: just as in the first article you were to consider yourself one of God's creatures and not doubt it, now you must think of yourself as one of the redeemed and never doubt that.

Emphasize one word above all others, for instance, Jesus Christ, *our* Lord. Likewise, suffered for *us*, died for *us*, arose for *us*. All this is ours and pertains to us; that *us* includes yourself, as the word of God declares.

Second, you must be sincerely grateful for such grace and rejoice in your salvation.

Third, you must sorrowfully lament and confess your wicked unbelief and mistrust of such a gift. Oh, what thoughts will come to mind—the idolatry you have practiced repeatedly, how much you have made of praying to the saints and of innumerable good works of yours which have opposed such salvation.

Fourth, pray now that God will preserve you from this time forward to the end in true and pure faith in Christ our Lord.

The Third Article of Sanctification

"I believe in the Holy Spirit," etc.

This is the third great light which teaches us where such a Creator and Redeemer may be found and plainly encountered in this world, and what this will all come to in the end. Much could be said about this, but here is a summary: Where the holy Christian church exists, there we can find God the Creator, God the Redeemer, God the Holy Spirit, that is, him who daily sanctifies us through the forgiveness of sins, etc. The church exists where the word of God concerning such faith is rightly preached and confessed.

Again you have occasion here to ponder long about everything that the Holy Spirit accomplishes in the church every day, etc.

Therefore be thankful that you have been called and have come into such a church.

Confess and lament your lack of faith and gratitude, that you have neglected all this, and pray for a true and steadfast faith that will remain and endure until you come to that place where all endures forever, that is, beyond the resurrection from the dead, in life eternal. Amen.

Notes

1. Probably Jerome's *Commentary on Matthew*, book 4 under Matthew 25:11. *Patrologia, Series Latina,* 221 vols. in 222, edited by J.P. Migne (Paris, 1844–1904), 26, 186.
2. 1 Thessalonians 5:17. Cf. Luke 11:9–13.
3. Exodus 20:7.
4. "His mischief returns upon his own head, and on his own pate his violence descends."
5. "Make haste, O God, to deliver me." Psalm 70:1.
6. "Make haste to help me, O Lord."
7. "Glory be to the Father and to the Son and to the Holy Ghost."
8. "Praise."
9. "Jot and tittle." Matthew 5:18 (KJV).
10. Literally, "nose," the idiom in Luther's day.
11. Ernst Thiele, *Luthers Sprichwörtersammlung* (Weimar, 1900), No. 213.
12. *Ibid.*
13. In enlarged editions, printed soon afterward, Luther added the section on the Apostles' Creed at this point, omitting the two following paragraphs.
14. In some early editions, Psalm 51 was inserted at this point.